Job Search Organizer

Track jobs you are applying to so that you keep ahead of the competition.

Job Log

Welcome to the Job Search Organizer where you can keep track of the jobs you are applying to so that you can keep ahead of the competition. There is a lot of information that you must remember in order to have a successful interview and so this organizer was created to help you through the process. The first few pages will help you track your skillset, jobs you've held in the past and any education or trainings you attend. By filling out these pages, you will have a quick reference when an interviewer asks about your history.

The next section allows you to list your references and contacts so that you can provide them if the hiring manager needs them to move forward in the hiring process. It also allows you a quick reference for when you need help and you can reach out to these people for ideas. There is also a section to write down your website logins so that you have a place to remember them all. As you search for job listings you'll come across many websites where you'll need to create accounts. This should help you log in quicker.

The next section is a list of some common interview questions. Prepare for your interview by answering these questions for yourself. Then when you're most likely asked these questions later, you'll already have a well thought out response and propel you ahead of the competition.

The final pages are for each job that you apply to. By using a template, you can compare jobs and make sure that you have all of the relevant information you need.

Thank you for purchasing the Job Search Organizer! Please leave a review on the seller's website and any suggestions of how to improve the organizer.

Skills

Write down your skills for quick reference.

Skill	Year Started Using	Years of Experience

Employment History

Write down your employment history for quick reference.

Dates	Position	Company
Supervisor	Company Address	Phone Number

Dates	Position	Company
Supervisor	Company Address	Phone Number

Dates	Position	Company
Supervisor	Company Address	Phone Number

Dates	Position	Company
Supervisor	Company Address	Phone Number

Dates	Position	Company
Supervisor	Company Address	Phone Number

Dates	Position	Company
Supervisor	Company Address	Phone Number

Dates	Position	Company
Supervisor	Company Address	Phone Number

Dates	Position	Company
Supervisor	Company Address	Phone Number

Education and Trainings

Write down any education and trainings you attended.

Course	Degree	School
Years	Address	Phone Number

Course	Degree	School
Years	Address	Phone Number

Course	Degree	School
Years	Address	Phone Number

Course	Degree	School
Years	Address	Phone Number

Course	Degree	School
Years	Address	Phone Number

Course	Degree	School
Years	Address	Phone Number

My Contacts & Network

List the people in your network that will help you in your job search. Include recruiters, job references and coaches.

Name   Email   Phone

Title/Role   Company

How do I know them?   What can they help with?

Name   Email   Phone

Title/Role   Company

How do I know them?   What can they help with?

Name   Email   Phone

Title/Role   Company

How do I know them?   What can they help with?

Name   Email   Phone

Title/Role   Company

How do I know them?   What can they help with?

Name   Email   Phone

Title/Role   Company

How do I know them?   What can they help with?

Website Logins

Write down your usernames and passwords so you can login quicker.

Username   Password

_____

_____

_____

_____

_____

_____

_____

_____

_____

_____

_____

_____

_____

_____

_____

_____

_____

_____

_____

_____

_____

_____

Common Job Interview Questions

Review some of the most common job interview questions below and prepare your answers so you're ready to give your best answer.

What are your greatest professional strengths?

What do you consider to be your weaknesses?

What do you consider to be your biggest professional achievement?

Tell me about the last time a co-worker or customer got angry with you. What happened?

Describe your dream job.

Why do you want to leave your current job?

What kind of work environment do you like best?

Tell me about the toughest decision you had to make in the last six months.

What is your leadership style?

Tell me about a time you disagreed with a decision. What did you do?

How would your boss and co-workers describe you?

What can we expect from you in your first three months?

Where do you see yourself in five years?

What are your salary requirements?

What do you like to do outside of work?

If you were an animal, which one would you want to be?

What steps would you take to make an important decision on the job?

Tell me about a time you had to relay bad news to a client or colleague.

What can you offer us that someone else can not?

Tell me about a time you made a mistake.

Would you work holidays/weekends?

Give a time when you went above and beyond the requirements for a project.

What was your biggest failure?

What motivates you?

Who's your mentor?

How do you handle pressure?

What are your career goals?

What gets you up in the morning?

Are you a leader or a follower?

What are your hobbies?

Position Title   Company Name   Glassdoor Rating

Date Applied   Deadline   Company Website

Salary   Address
$

Source/Reference #   Commute Time
                                                                       hh   mm

Website Login
u: p:
                                                                       ☐ Posted Directly
                                                                       ☐ Posted by Agency

Interviews

1 Date & Time   Location   Contact

Questions to Ask During Interview & Notes for Follow-Up
                                                ☐ Thank You Note Sent

2 Date & Time   Location   Contact

Questions to Ask During Interview & Notes for Follow-Up

3 Date & Time   Location   Contact

Questions to Ask During Interview & Notes for Follow-Up

Contacts for this Role

Name	Email	Phone
Title/Role	Company	

Name	Email	Phone
Title/Role	Company	

Name	Email	Phone
Title/Role	Company	

Name	Email	Phone
Title/Role	Company	

Notes, Feedback, Reflection, Any Questions that Need Followup

Position Title   Company Name   Glassdoor Rating

Date Applied   Deadline   Company Website

Salary   Address
$

Source/Reference #   Commute Time
                                                                 hh   mm

Website Login
u: p:
                                                                 ☐ Posted Directly
                                                                 ☐ Posted by Agency

Interviews

1 Date & Time   Location   Contact

Questions to Ask During Interview & Notes for Follow-Up

                                                    ☐ Thank You Note Sent

2 Date & Time   Location   Contact

Questions to Ask During Interview & Notes for Follow-Up

3 Date & Time   Location   Contact

Questions to Ask During Interview & Notes for Follow-Up

Contacts for this Role

Name	Email	Phone
Title/Role	Company	

Name	Email	Phone
Title/Role	Company	

Name	Email	Phone
Title/Role	Company	

Name	Email	Phone
Title/Role	Company	

Notes, Feedback, Reflection, Any Questions that Need Followup

Position Title   Company Name   Glassdoor Rating

Date Applied   Deadline   Company Website

Salary   Address
$

Source/Reference #   Commute Time
                                                                        hh   mm

Website Login
u: p: ☐ Posted Directly
                                                                     ☐ Posted by Agency

Interviews

1 Date & Time   Location   Contact

Questions to Ask During Interview & Notes for Follow-Up
                                                ☐ Thank You Note Sent

2 Date & Time   Location   Contact

Questions to Ask During Interview & Notes for Follow-Up

3 Date & Time   Location   Contact

Questions to Ask During Interview & Notes for Follow-Up

Contacts for this Role

Name	Email	Phone
Title/Role	Company	

Name	Email	Phone
Title/Role	Company	

Name	Email	Phone
Title/Role	Company	

Name	Email	Phone
Title/Role	Company	

Notes, Feedback, Reflection, Any Questions that Need Followup

(1)	(2)	(3)	(4)	(5)	(6)	(7)	(8)	(9)
Application Sent	Follow Up Sent	Interview 1	Thank You Sent	Interview 2	Interview 3	Offer Received	Rejected	Accepted

Position Title   Company Name   Glassdoor Rating

Date Applied   Deadline   Company Website

Salary   Address
$

Source/Reference #   Commute Time
                                                          hh   mm

Website Login
u: p: ☐ Posted Directly
                                                          ☐ Posted by Agency

Interviews

1 Date & Time   Location   Contact

Questions to Ask During Interview & Notes for Follow-Up
                                    ☐ Thank You Note Sent

2 Date & Time   Location   Contact

Questions to Ask During Interview & Notes for Follow-Up

3 Date & Time   Location   Contact

Questions to Ask During Interview & Notes for Follow-Up

Contacts for this Role

Name	Email	Phone
Title/Role	Company	

Name	Email	Phone
Title/Role	Company	

Name	Email	Phone
Title/Role	Company	

Name	Email	Phone
Title/Role	Company	

Notes, Feedback, Reflection, Any Questions that Need Followup

Position Title   Company Name   Glassdoor Rating

Date Applied   Deadline   Company Website

Salary   Address
$

Source/Reference #   Commute Time
                                                                        hh   mm

Website Login
u: p:
                                                                        ☐ Posted Directly
                                                                        ☐ Posted by Agency

Interviews

1 Date & Time   Location   Contact

Questions to Ask During Interview & Notes for Follow-Up

                                                    ☐ Thank You Note Sent

2 Date & Time   Location   Contact

Questions to Ask During Interview & Notes for Follow-Up

3 Date & Time   Location   Contact

Questions to Ask During Interview & Notes for Follow-Up

Contacts for this Role

Name	Email	Phone
Title/Role	Company	

Name	Email	Phone
Title/Role	Company	

Name	Email	Phone
Title/Role	Company	

Name	Email	Phone
Title/Role	Company	

Notes, Feedback, Reflection, Any Questions that Need Followup

(1)──(2)──(3)──(4)──(5)──(6)──(7)──(8)──(9)
Application Sent   Follow Up Sent   Interview 1   Thank You Sent   Interview 2   Interview 3   Offer Received   Rejected   Accepted

Position Title   Company Name   Glassdoor Rating

Date Applied   Deadline   Company Website

Salary   Address
$

Source/Reference #   Commute Time
                                                         hh   mm

Website Login
u: p: ☐ Posted Directly
                                                         ☐ Posted by Agency

Interviews

1   Date & Time   Location   Contact

Questions to Ask During Interview & Notes for Follow-Up

                                                    ☐ Thank You Note Sent

2   Date & Time   Location   Contact

Questions to Ask During Interview & Notes for Follow-Up

3   Date & Time   Location   Contact

Questions to Ask During Interview & Notes for Follow-Up

Contacts for this Role

Name	Email	Phone
Title/Role	Company	

Name	Email	Phone
Title/Role	Company	

Name	Email	Phone
Title/Role	Company	

Name	Email	Phone
Title/Role	Company	

Notes, Feedback, Reflection, Any Questions that Need Followup

Position Title   Company Name   Glassdoor Rating

Date Applied   Deadline   Company Website

Salary   Address
$

Source/Reference #   Commute Time
                                                                              hh   mm

Website Login
u: p: ☐ Posted Directly
                                                                            ☐ Posted by Agency

Interviews

1 Date & Time   Location   Contact

Questions to Ask During Interview & Notes for Follow-Up
                                                  ☐ Thank You Note Sent

2 Date & Time   Location   Contact

Questions to Ask During Interview & Notes for Follow-Up

3 Date & Time   Location   Contact

Questions to Ask During Interview & Notes for Follow-Up

Contents for this Role

Name	Email	Phone
Title/Role	Company	

Name	Email	Phone
Title/Role	Company	

Name	Email	Phone
Title/Role	Company	

Name	Email	Phone
Title/Role	Company	

Notes, Feedback, Reflection, Any Questions that Need Followup

Position Title   Company Name   Glassdoor Rating

Date Applied   Deadline   Company Website

Salary   Address
$

Source/Reference #   Commute Time
                                                                 hh   mm

Website Login
u: p: ☐ Posted Directly
                                                                 ☐ Posted by Agency

Interviews

1   Date & Time   Location   Contact

Questions to Ask During Interview & Notes for Follow-Up
                                                  ☐ Thank You Note Sent

2   Date & Time   Location   Contact

Questions to Ask During Interview & Notes for Follow-Up

3   Date & Time   Location   Contact

Questions to Ask During Interview & Notes for Follow-Up

Contacts for this Role

Name	Email	Phone
Title/Role	Company	

Name	Email	Phone
Title/Role	Company	

Name	Email	Phone
Title/Role	Company	

Name	Email	Phone
Title/Role	Company	

Notes, Feedback, Reflection, Any Questions that Need Followup

Position Title   Company Name   Glassdoor Rating

Date Applied   Deadline   Company Website

Salary   Address
$

Source/Reference #   Commute Time
                                                                              hh   mm

Website Login
u: p:
                                                                         ☐ Posted Directly

                                                                         ☐ Posted by Agency

Interviews

1   Date & Time   Location   Contact

Questions to Ask During Interview & Notes for Follow-Up

                                                   ☐ Thank You Note Sent

2   Date & Time   Location   Contact

Questions to Ask During Interview & Notes for Follow-Up

3   Date & Time   Location   Contact

Questions to Ask During Interview & Notes for Follow-Up

Contacts for this Role

Name   Email   Phone

Title/Role   Company

Name   Email   Phone

Title/Role   Company

Name   Email   Phone

Title/Role   Company

Name   Email   Phone

Title/Role   Company

Notes, Feedback, Reflection, Any Questions that Need Followup

1	2	3	4	5	6	7	8	9
Application Sent	Follow Up Sent	Interview 1	Thank You Sent	Interview 2	Interview 3	Offer Received	Rejected	Accepted

Position Title   Company Name   Glassdoor Rating

Date Applied   Deadline   Company Website

Salary   Address
$

Source/Reference #   Commute Time
                                                                       hh   mm

Website Login
u: p:
                                                                   ☐ Posted Directly
                                                                   ☐ Posted by Agency

Interviews

1 Date & Time   Location   Contact

Questions to Ask During Interview & Notes for Follow-Up
                                                  ☐ Thank You Note Sent

2 Date & Time   Location   Contact

Questions to Ask During Interview & Notes for Follow-Up

3 Date & Time   Location   Contact

Questions to Ask During Interview & Notes for Follow-Up

Contents for this Role

Name	Email	Phone
Title/Role	Company	

Name	Email	Phone
Title/Role	Company	

Name	Email	Phone
Title/Role	Company	

Name	Email	Phone
Title/Role	Company	

Notes, Feedback, Reflection, Any Questions that Need Followup

(1)	—	(2)	—	(3)	—	(4)	—	(5)	—	(6)	—	(7)	—	(8)	—	(9)
Application Sent		Follow Up Sent		Interview 1		Thank You Sent		Interview 2		Interview 3		Offer Received		Rejected		Accepted

Position Title   Company Name   Glassdoor Rating

Date Applied   Deadline   Company Website

Salary
$ Address

Source/Reference #   Commute Time
                                                          hh   mm

Website Login
u: p:
                                                          ☐ Posted Directly
                                                          ☐ Posted by Agency

Interviews

1 Date & Time   Location   Contact

Questions to Ask During Interview & Notes for Follow-Up
                                    ☐ Thank You Note Sent

2 Date & Time   Location   Contact

Questions to Ask During Interview & Notes for Follow-Up

3 Date & Time   Location   Contact

Questions to Ask During Interview & Notes for Follow-Up

Contacts for this Role

Name	Email	Phone
Title/Role	Company	

Name	Email	Phone
Title/Role	Company	

Name	Email	Phone
Title/Role	Company	

Name	Email	Phone
Title/Role	Company	

Notes, Feedback, Reflection, Any Questions that Need Followup

Position Title   Company Name   Glassdoor Rating

Date Applied   Deadline   Company Website

Salary   Address
$

Source/Reference #   Commute Time
                                                              hh   mm

Website Login
u: p:
                                                              ☐ Posted Directly
                                                              ☐ Posted by Agency

Interviews

1 Date & Time   Location   Contact

Questions to Ask During Interview & Notes for Follow-Up

                                        ☐ Thank You Note Sent

2 Date & Time   Location   Contact

Questions to Ask During Interview & Notes for Follow-Up

3 Date & Time   Location   Contact

Questions to Ask During Interview & Notes for Follow-Up

Contacts for this Role

Name	Email	Phone
Title/Role	Company	

Name	Email	Phone
Title/Role	Company	

Name	Email	Phone
Title/Role	Company	

Name	Email	Phone
Title/Role	Company	

Notes, Feedback, Reflection, Any Questions that Need Followup

Position Title   Company Name   Glassdoor Rating

Date Applied   Deadline   Company Website

Salary   Address
$

Source/Reference #   Commute Time
                                                                     hh   mm

Website Login
u: p: ☐ Posted Directly
                                                                   ☐ Posted by Agency

Interviews

1 Date & Time   Location   Contact

Questions to Ask During Interview & Notes for Follow-Up
                                                    ☐ Thank You Note Sent

2 Date & Time   Location   Contact

Questions to Ask During Interview & Notes for Follow-Up

3 Date & Time   Location   Contact

Questions to Ask During Interview & Notes for Follow-Up

Contacts for this Role

Name	Email	Phone
Title/Role	Company	

Name	Email	Phone
Title/Role	Company	

Name	Email	Phone
Title/Role	Company	

Name	Email	Phone
Title/Role	Company	

Notes, Feedback, Reflection, Any Questions that Need Followup

Position Title   Company Name   Glassdoor Rating

Date Applied   Deadline   Company Website

Salary   Address
$

Source/Reference #   Commute Time
                                                                hh   mm

Website Login
u: p:
                                                                ☐ Posted Directly
                                                                ☐ Posted by Agency

Interviews

1 Date & Time   Location   Contact

Questions to Ask During Interview & Notes for Follow-Up

                                                  ☐ Thank You Note Sent

2 Date & Time   Location   Contact

Questions to Ask During Interview & Notes for Follow-Up

3 Date & Time   Location   Contact

Questions to Ask During Interview & Notes for Follow-Up

Contacts for this Role

Name	Email	Phone
Title/Role	Company	

Name	Email	Phone
Title/Role	Company	

Name	Email	Phone
Title/Role	Company	

Name	Email	Phone
Title/Role	Company	

Notes, Feedback, Reflection, Any Questions that Need Followup

(1) ———— (2) ———— (3) ———— (4) ———— (5) ———— (6) ———— (7) ———— (8) ———— (9)

Application Sent   Follow Up Sent   Interview 1   Thank You Sent   Interview 2   Interview 3   Offer Received   Rejected   Accepted

Position Title   Company Name   Glassdoor Rating

Date Applied   Deadline   Company Website

Salary
$
         Address

Source/Reference #   Commute Time
         hh   mm

Website Login
u: p:

☐ Posted Directly

☐ Posted by Agency

Interviews

1 Date & Time   Location   Contact

Questions to Ask During Interview & Notes for Follow-Up

☐ Thank You Note Sent

2 Date & Time   Location   Contact

Questions to Ask During Interview & Notes for Follow-Up

3 Date & Time   Location   Contact

Questions to Ask During Interview & Notes for Follow-Up

Contacts for this Role

Name	Email	Phone
Title/Role	Company	

Name	Email	Phone
Title/Role	Company	

Name	Email	Phone
Title/Role	Company	

Name	Email	Phone
Title/Role	Company	

Notes, Feedback, Reflection, Any Questions that Need Followup

Position Title   Company Name   Glassdoor Rating

Date Applied   Deadline   Company Website

Salary   Address
$

Source/Reference #   Commute Time
                                                                     hh   mm

Website Login
u: p:
                                                                     ☐ Posted Directly
                                                                     ☐ Posted by Agency

Interviews

1 Date & Time   Location   Contact

Questions to Ask During Interview & Notes for Follow-Up
                                                    ☐ Thank You Note Sent

2 Date & Time   Location   Contact

Questions to Ask During Interview & Notes for Follow-Up

3 Date & Time   Location   Contact

Questions to Ask During Interview & Notes for Follow-Up

Contents for this Role

Name	Email	Phone
Title/Role	Company	

Name	Email	Phone
Title/Role	Company	

Name	Email	Phone
Title/Role	Company	

Name	Email	Phone
Title/Role	Company	

Notes, Feedback, Reflection, Any Questions that Need Followup

Position Title   Company Name   Glassdoor Rating

Date Applied   Deadline   Company Website

Salary   Address
$

Source/Reference #   Commute Time
                                                                 hh   mm

Website Login
u: p: ☐ Posted Directly

                                                                 ☐ Posted by Agency

Interviews

1 Date & Time   Location   Contact

Questions to Ask During Interview & Notes for Follow-Up

                                        ☐ Thank You Note Sent

2 Date & Time   Location   Contact

Questions to Ask During Interview & Notes for Follow-Up

3 Date & Time   Location   Contact

Questions to Ask During Interview & Notes for Follow-Up

Contacts for this Role

Name	Email	Phone
Title/Role	Company	

Name	Email	Phone
Title/Role	Company	

Name	Email	Phone
Title/Role	Company	

Name	Email	Phone
Title/Role	Company	

Notes, Feedback, Reflection, Any Questions that Need Followup

①——②——③——④——⑤——⑥——⑦——⑧——⑨
Application Sent Follow Up Sent Interview 1 Thank You Sent Interview 2 Interview 3 Offer Received Rejected Accepted

Position Title   Company Name   Glassdoor Rating

Date Applied   Deadline   Company Website

Salary   Address
$

Source/Reference #   Commute Time
                                                                          hh   mm

Website Login
u: p: ☐ Posted Directly
                                                                      ☐ Posted by Agency

Interviews

1 Date & Time   Location   Contact

Questions to Ask During Interview & Notes for Follow-Up
                                                        ☐ Thank You Note Sent

2 Date & Time   Location   Contact

Questions to Ask During Interview & Notes for Follow-Up

3 Date & Time   Location   Contact

Questions to Ask During Interview & Notes for Follow-Up

Contacts for this Role

Name	Email	Phone
Title/Role	Company	

Name	Email	Phone
Title/Role	Company	

Name	Email	Phone
Title/Role	Company	

Name	Email	Phone
Title/Role	Company	

Notes, Feedback, Reflection, Any Questions that Need Followup

Position Title   Company Name   Glassdoor Rating

Date Applied   Deadline   Company Website

Salary   Address
$

Source/Reference #   Commute Time
                                                                     hh   mm

Website Login
u: p:
                                                                     ☐ Posted Directly
                                                                     ☐ Posted by Agency

Interviews

1 Date & Time   Location   Contact

Questions to Ask During Interview & Notes for Follow-Up

                                             ☐ Thank You Note Sent

2 Date & Time   Location   Contact

Questions to Ask During Interview & Notes for Follow-Up

3 Date & Time   Location   Contact

Questions to Ask During Interview & Notes for Follow-Up

Contacts for this Role

Name	Email	Phone
Title/Role	Company	

Name	Email	Phone
Title/Role	Company	

Name	Email	Phone
Title/Role	Company	

Name	Email	Phone
Title/Role	Company	

Notes, Feedback, Reflection, Any Questions that Need Followup

Position Title   Company Name   Glassdoor Rating

Date Applied   Deadline   Company Website

Salary   Address
$

Source/Reference #   Commute Time
                                                                  hh   mm

Website Login
u: p: ☐ Posted Directly
                                                                  ☐ Posted by Agency

Interviews

1 Date & Time   Location   Contact

Questions to Ask During Interview & Notes for Follow-Up

                                              ☐ Thank You Note Sent

2 Date & Time   Location   Contact

Questions to Ask During Interview & Notes for Follow-Up

3 Date & Time   Location   Contact

Questions to Ask During Interview & Notes for Follow-Up

Contacts for this Role

Name	Email	Phone
Title/Role	Company	

Name	Email	Phone
Title/Role	Company	

Name	Email	Phone
Title/Role	Company	

Name	Email	Phone
Title/Role	Company	

Notes, Feedback, Reflection, Any Questions that Need Followup

(1)	(2)	(3)	(4)	(5)	(6)	(7)	(8)	(9)
Application Sent	Follow Up Sent	Interview 1	Thank You Sent	Interview 2	Interview 3	Offer Received	Rejected	Accepted

Position Title   Company Name   Glassdoor Rating

Date Applied   Deadline   Company Website

Salary   Address
$

Source/Reference #   Commute Time
                                                                  hh   mm

Website Login
u: p:

                                                                  ☐ Posted Directly
                                                                  ☐ Posted by Agency

Interviews

1 Date & Time   Location   Contact

Questions to Ask During Interview & Notes for Follow-Up
                                                  ☐ Thank You Note Sent

2 Date & Time   Location   Contact

Questions to Ask During Interview & Notes for Follow-Up

3 Date & Time   Location   Contact

Questions to Ask During Interview & Notes for Follow-Up

Contacts for this Role

Name	Email	Phone
Title/Role	Company	

Name	Email	Phone
Title/Role	Company	

Name	Email	Phone
Title/Role	Company	

Name	Email	Phone
Title/Role	Company	

Notes, Feedback, Reflection, Any Questions that Need Followup

Position Title　　　　　Company Name　　　　　Glassdoor Rating

Date Applied　　　　　Deadline　　　　　　　Company Website

Salary　　　　　　　　Address
$

Source/Reference #　　　　　　　　　　　　Commute Time
　　　　　　　　　　　　　　　　　　　　　hh　　　mm

Website Login
u:　　　　　　　p:
　　　　　　　　　　　　　　　　　　　☐ Posted Directly
　　　　　　　　　　　　　　　　　　　☐ Posted by Agency

Interviews

1　Date & Time　　　　Location　　　　　Contact

Questions to Ask During Interview & Notes for Follow-Up
　　　　　　　　　　　　　　　　　☐ Thank You Note Sent

2　Date & Time　　　　Location　　　　　Contact

Questions to Ask During Interview & Notes for Follow-Up

3　Date & Time　　　　Location　　　　　Contact

Questions to Ask During Interview & Notes for Follow-Up

Contacts for this Role

Name	Email	Phone
Title/Role	Company	

Name	Email	Phone
Title/Role	Company	

Name	Email	Phone
Title/Role	Company	

Name	Email	Phone
Title/Role	Company	

Notes, Feedback, Reflection, Any Questions that Need Followup

Position Title   Company Name   Glassdoor Rating

Date Applied   Deadline   Company Website

Salary   Address
$

Source/Reference #   Commute Time
                                                             hh   mm

Website Login
u: p: ☐ Posted Directly
                                                         ☐ Posted by Agency

Interviews

---

1 Date & Time   Location   Contact

Questions to Ask During Interview & Notes for Follow-Up
                                                ☐ Thank You Note Sent

---

2 Date & Time   Location   Contact

Questions to Ask During Interview & Notes for Follow-Up

---

3 Date & Time   Location   Contact

Questions to Ask During Interview & Notes for Follow-Up

Contacts for this Role

Name	Email	Phone
Title/Role	Company	

Name	Email	Phone
Title/Role	Company	

Name	Email	Phone
Title/Role	Company	

Name	Email	Phone
Title/Role	Company	

Notes, Feedback, Reflection, Any Questions that Need Followup

Position Title   Company Name   Glassdoor Rating

Date Applied   Deadline   Company Website

Salary   Address
$

Source/Reference #   Commute Time
                                                                 hh   mm

Website Login
u: p:
                                                                 ☐ Posted Directly
                                                                 ☐ Posted by Agency

Interviews

1 Date & Time   Location   Contact

Questions to Ask During Interview & Notes for Follow-Up

                                                 ☐ Thank You Note Sent

2 Date & Time   Location   Contact

Questions to Ask During Interview & Notes for Follow-Up

3 Date & Time   Location   Contact

Questions to Ask During Interview & Notes for Follow-Up

Contacts for this Role

Name	Email	Phone
Title/Role	Company	

Name	Email	Phone
Title/Role	Company	

Name	Email	Phone
Title/Role	Company	

Name	Email	Phone
Title/Role	Company	

Notes, Feedback, Reflection, Any Questions that Need Followup

```
 (1)──(2)──(3)──(4)──(5)──(6)──(7)──(8)──(9)
```
Application Sent   Follow Up Sent   Interview 1   Thank You Sent   Interview 2   Interview 3   Offer Received   Rejected   Accepted

Position Title   Company Name   Glassdoor Rating

Date Applied   Deadline   Company Website

Salary   Address
$

Source/Reference #   Commute Time
                                                                        hh   mm

Website Login
u: p:
                                                                        ☐ Posted Directly
                                                                        ☐ Posted by Agency

Interviews

───
1 Date & Time   Location   Contact

Questions to Ask During Interview & Notes for Follow-Up
                                                    ☐ Thank You Note Sent

───
2 Date & Time   Location   Contact

Questions to Ask During Interview & Notes for Follow-Up

───
3 Date & Time   Location   Contact

Questions to Ask During Interview & Notes for Follow-Up

Contacts for this Role

Name	Email	Phone
Title/Role	Company	

Name	Email	Phone
Title/Role	Company	

Name	Email	Phone
Title/Role	Company	

Name	Email	Phone
Title/Role	Company	

Notes, Feedback, Reflection, Any Questions that Need Followup

Position Title   Company Name   Glassdoor Rating

Date Applied   Deadline   Company Website

Salary   Address
$

Source/Reference #   Commute Time
                                                                    hh   mm

Website Login
u: p: ☐ Posted Directly
                                                                    ☐ Posted by Agency

Interviews

1 Date & Time   Location   Contact

Questions to Ask During Interview & Notes for Follow-Up

                                                  ☐ Thank You Note Sent

2 Date & Time   Location   Contact

Questions to Ask During Interview & Notes for Follow-Up

3 Date & Time   Location   Contact

Questions to Ask During Interview & Notes for Follow-Up

Contents for this Role

Name	Email	Phone
Title/Role	Company	

Name	Email	Phone
Title/Role	Company	

Name	Email	Phone
Title/Role	Company	

Name	Email	Phone
Title/Role	Company	

Notes, Feedback, Reflection, Any Questions that Need Followup

(1)	(2)	(3)	(4)	(5)	(6)	(7)	(8)	(9)
Application Sent	Follow Up Sent	Interview 1	Thank You Sent	Interview 2	Interview 3	Offer Received	Rejected	Accepted

Position Title   Company Name   Glassdoor Rating

Date Applied   Deadline   Company Website

Salary   Address
$

Source/Reference #   Commute Time
                                                                            hh   mm

Website Login
u: p: ☐ Posted Directly
                                                                            ☐ Posted by Agency

Interviews

---

1 Date & Time   Location   Contact

Questions to Ask During Interview & Notes for Follow-Up

                                                ☐ Thank You Note Sent

---

2 Date & Time   Location   Contact

Questions to Ask During Interview & Notes for Follow-Up

---

3 Date & Time   Location   Contact

Questions to Ask During Interview & Notes for Follow-Up

Contacts for this Role

Name	Email	Phone
Title/Role	Company	

Name	Email	Phone
Title/Role	Company	

Name	Email	Phone
Title/Role	Company	

Name	Email	Phone
Title/Role	Company	

Notes, Feedback, Reflection, Any Questions that Need Followup

1	—	2	—	3	—	4	—	5	—	6	—	7	—	8	—	9
Application Sent		Follow Up Sent		Interview 1		Thank You Sent		Interview 2		Interview 3		Offer Received		Rejected		Accepted

Position Title   Company Name   Glassdoor Rating

Date Applied   Deadline   Company Website

Salary   Address
$

Source/Reference #   Commute Time
                                                                  hh   mm

Website Login
u: p:
                                                                  ☐ Posted Directly
                                                                  ☐ Posted by Agency

Interviews

1 Date & Time   Location   Contact

Questions to Ask During Interview & Notes for Follow-Up

                                                ☐ Thank You Note Sent

2 Date & Time   Location   Contact

Questions to Ask During Interview & Notes for Follow-Up

3 Date & Time   Location   Contact

Questions to Ask During Interview & Notes for Follow-Up

Contacts for this Role

Name	Email	Phone
Title/Role	Company	

Name	Email	Phone
Title/Role	Company	

Name	Email	Phone
Title/Role	Company	

Name	Email	Phone
Title/Role	Company	

Notes, Feedback, Reflection, Any Questions that Need Followup

① — ② — ③ — ④ — ⑤ — ⑥ — ⑦ — ⑧ — ⑨

Application Sent   Follow Up Sent   Interview 1   Thank You Sent   Interview 2   Interview 3   Offer Received   Rejected   Accepted

Position Title   Company Name   Glassdoor Rating

Date Applied   Deadline   Company Website

Salary   Address
$

Source/Reference #   Commute Time
                                                                  hh   mm

Website Login
u: p:
                                                                  ☐ Posted Directly
                                                                  ☐ Posted by Agency

Interviews

1 Date & Time   Location   Contact

Questions to Ask During Interview & Notes for Follow-Up

                                                 ☐ Thank You Note Sent

2 Date & Time   Location   Contact

Questions to Ask During Interview & Notes for Follow-Up

3 Date & Time   Location   Contact

Questions to Ask During Interview & Notes for Follow-Up

Contacts for this Role

Name	Email	Phone
Title/Role	Company	

Name	Email	Phone
Title/Role	Company	

Name	Email	Phone
Title/Role	Company	

Name	Email	Phone
Title/Role	Company	

Notes, Feedback, Reflection, Any Questions that Need Followup

①————	②————	③————	④————	⑤————	⑥————	⑦————	⑧————	⑨
Application Sent	Follow Up Sent	Interview 1	Thank You Sent	Interview 2	Interview 3	Offer Received	Rejected	Accepted

Position Title   Company Name   Glassdoor Rating

Date Applied   Deadline   Company Website

Salary   Address
$

Source/Reference #   Commute Time
                                                                        hh   mm

Website Login
u: p:
                                                                   ☐ Posted Directly
                                                                   ☐ Posted by Agency

Interviews

1 Date & Time   Location   Contact

Questions to Ask During Interview & Notes for Follow-Up
                                                     ☐ Thank You Note Sent

2 Date & Time   Location   Contact

Questions to Ask During Interview & Notes for Follow-Up

3 Date & Time   Location   Contact

Questions to Ask During Interview & Notes for Follow-Up

Contacts for this Role

Name	Email	Phone
Title/Role	Company	

Name	Email	Phone
Title/Role	Company	

Name	Email	Phone
Title/Role	Company	

Name	Email	Phone
Title/Role	Company	

Notes, Feedback, Reflection, Any Questions that Need Followup

| ①————② | ③————④ | ⑤————⑥ | ⑦————⑧ | ⑨ |

(1)	(2)	(3)	(4)	(5)	(6)	(7)	(8)	(9)
Application Sent	Follow Up Sent	Interview 1	Thank You Sent	Interview 2	Interview 3	Offer Received	Rejected	Accepted

Position Title   Company Name   Glassdoor Rating

Date Applied   Deadline   Company Website

Salary   Address
$

Source/Reference #   Commute Time
                                                                              hh   mm

Website Login
u: p:
                                                                         ☐ Posted Directly
                                                                         ☐ Posted by Agency

Interviews

1 Date & Time   Location   Contact

Questions to Ask During Interview & Notes for Follow-Up
                                                ☐ Thank You Note Sent

2 Date & Time   Location   Contact

Questions to Ask During Interview & Notes for Follow-Up

3 Date & Time   Location   Contact

Questions to Ask During Interview & Notes for Follow-Up

Contacts for this Role

Name	Email	Phone

| Title/Role | Company | |

Name	Email	Phone

| Title/Role | Company | |

Name	Email	Phone

| Title/Role | Company | |

Name	Email	Phone

| Title/Role | Company | |

Notes, Feedback, Reflection, Any Questions that Need Followup

①	②	③	④	⑤	⑥	⑦	⑧	⑨
Application Sent	Follow Up Sent	Interview 1	Thank You Sent	Interview 2	Interview 3	Offer Received	Rejected	Accepted

Position Title   Company Name   Glassdoor Rating

Date Applied   Deadline   Company Website

Salary   Address
$

Source/Reference #   Commute Time
        hh mm

Website Login
u: p: ☐ Posted Directly
        ☐ Posted by Agency

Interviews

1 Date & Time   Location   Contact

Questions to Ask During Interview & Notes for Follow-Up
        ☐ Thank You Note Sent

2 Date & Time   Location   Contact

Questions to Ask During Interview & Notes for Follow-Up

3 Date & Time   Location   Contact

Questions to Ask During Interview & Notes for Follow-Up

Contacts for this Role

Name	Email	Phone
Title/Role	Company	

Name	Email	Phone
Title/Role	Company	

Name	Email	Phone
Title/Role	Company	

Name	Email	Phone
Title/Role	Company	

Notes, Feedback, Reflection, Any Questions that Need Followup

Position Title   Company Name   Glassdoor Rating

Date Applied   Deadline   Company Website

Salary   Address
$

Source/Reference #   Commute Time
                                                                              hh   mm

Website Login
u: p:
                                                                         ☐ Posted Directly
                                                                         ☐ Posted by Agency

Interviews

1 Date & Time   Location   Contact

Questions to Ask During Interview & Notes for Follow-Up
                                                    ☐ Thank You Note Sent

2 Date & Time   Location   Contact

Questions to Ask During Interview & Notes for Follow-Up

3 Date & Time   Location   Contact

Questions to Ask During Interview & Notes for Follow-Up

Contacts for this Role

Name	Email	Phone
Title/Role	Company	

Name	Email	Phone
Title/Role	Company	

Name	Email	Phone
Title/Role	Company	

Name	Email	Phone
Title/Role	Company	

Notes, Feedback, Reflection, Any Questions that Need Followup

Position Title   Company Name   Glassdoor Rating

Date Applied   Deadline   Company Website

Salary   Address
$

Source/Reference #   Commute Time
                                                                            hh   mm

Website Login
u: p:
                                                                  ☐ Posted Directly
                                                                  ☐ Posted by Agency

Interviews

1 Date & Time   Location   Contact

Questions to Ask During Interview & Notes for Follow-Up
                                              ☐ Thank You Note Sent

2 Date & Time   Location   Contact

Questions to Ask During Interview & Notes for Follow-Up

3 Date & Time   Location   Contact

Questions to Ask During Interview & Notes for Follow-Up

Contacts for this Role

Name	Email	Phone
Title/Role	Company	

Name	Email	Phone
Title/Role	Company	

Name	Email	Phone
Title/Role	Company	

Name	Email	Phone
Title/Role	Company	

Notes, Feedback, Reflection, Any Questions that Need Followup

Position Title   Company Name   Glassdoor Rating

Date Applied   Deadline   Company Website

Salary   Address
$

Source/Reference #   Commute Time
                                                                    hh   mm

Website Login
u: p: ☐ Posted Directly
                                                                 ☐ Posted by Agency

Interviews

1 Date & Time   Location   Contact

Questions to Ask During Interview & Notes for Follow-Up

                                              ☐ Thank You Note Sent

2 Date & Time   Location   Contact

Questions to Ask During Interview & Notes for Follow-Up

3 Date & Time   Location   Contact

Questions to Ask During Interview & Notes for Follow-Up

Contacts for this Role

Name	Email	Phone
Title/Role	Company	

Name	Email	Phone
Title/Role	Company	

Name	Email	Phone
Title/Role	Company	

Name	Email	Phone
Title/Role	Company	

Notes, Feedback, Reflection, Any Questions that Need Followup

(1)—(2)—(3)—(4)—(5)—(6)—(7)—(8)—(9)

Application Sent   Follow Up Sent   Interview 1   Thank You Sent   Interview 2   Interview 3   Offer Received   Rejected   Accepted

Position Title   Company Name   Glassdoor Rating

Date Applied   Deadline   Company Website

Salary   Address
$

Source/Reference #   Commute Time
                                                                       hh   mm

Website Login
u: p:
                                                                       ☐ Posted Directly
                                                                       ☐ Posted by Agency

Interviews

1   Date & Time   Location   Contact

Questions to Ask During Interview & Notes for Follow-Up

                                                   ☐ Thank You Note Sent

2   Date & Time   Location   Contact

Questions to Ask During Interview & Notes for Follow-Up

3   Date & Time   Location   Contact

Questions to Ask During Interview & Notes for Follow-Up

Contacts for this Role

Name	Email	Phone
Title/Role	Company	

Name	Email	Phone
Title/Role	Company	

Name	Email	Phone
Title/Role	Company	

Name	Email	Phone
Title/Role	Company	

Notes, Feedback, Reflection, Any Questions that Need Followup

(1)	(2)	(3)	(4)	(5)	(6)	(7)	(8)	(9)
Application Sent	Follow Up Sent	Interview 1	Thank You Sent	Interview 2	Interview 3	Offer Received	Rejected	Accepted

Position Title   Company Name   Glassdoor Rating

Date Applied   Deadline   Company Website

Salary   Address
$

Source/Reference #   Commute Time
                                                                        hh   mm

Website Login
u: p:
                                                                        ☐ Posted Directly
                                                                        ☐ Posted by Agency

Interviews

1 Date & Time   Location   Contact

Questions to Ask During Interview & Notes for Follow-Up
                                                                ☐ Thank You Note Sent

2 Date & Time   Location   Contact

Questions to Ask During Interview & Notes for Follow-Up

3 Date & Time   Location   Contact

Questions to Ask During Interview & Notes for Follow-Up

Contacts for this Role

Name	Email	Phone
Title/Role	Company	

Name	Email	Phone
Title/Role	Company	

Name	Email	Phone
Title/Role	Company	

Name	Email	Phone
Title/Role	Company	

Notes, Feedback, Reflection, Any Questions that Need Followup

Position Title   Company Name   Glassdoor Rating

Date Applied   Deadline   Company Website

Salary   Address
$

Source/Reference #   Commute Time
                                                                  hh   mm

Website Login
u: p:
                                                                  ☐ Posted Directly
                                                                  ☐ Posted by Agency

Interviews

1 Date & Time   Location   Contact

Questions to Ask During Interview & Notes for Follow-Up
                                                      ☐ Thank You Note Sent

2 Date & Time   Location   Contact

Questions to Ask During Interview & Notes for Follow-Up

3 Date & Time   Location   Contact

Questions to Ask During Interview & Notes for Follow-Up

Contacts for this Role

Name	Email	Phone
Title/Role	Company	

Name	Email	Phone
Title/Role	Company	

Name	Email	Phone
Title/Role	Company	

Name	Email	Phone
Title/Role	Company	

Notes, Feedback, Reflection, Any Questions that Need Followup

(1)	(2)	(3)	(4)	(5)	(6)	(7)	(8)	(9)
Application Sent	Follow Up Sent	Interview 1	Thank You Sent	Interview 2	Interview 3	Offer Received	Rejected	Accepted

Position Title   Company Name   Glassdoor Rating

Date Applied   Deadline   Company Website

Salary   Address
$

Source/Reference #   Commute Time
                                                                                 hh   mm

Website Login
u: p:
                                                                             ☐ Posted Directly
                                                                             ☐ Posted by Agency

Interviews

1 Date & Time   Location   Contact

Questions to Ask During Interview & Notes for Follow-Up

☐ Thank You Note Sent

2 Date & Time   Location   Contact

Questions to Ask During Interview & Notes for Follow-Up

3 Date & Time   Location   Contact

Questions to Ask During Interview & Notes for Follow-Up

Contents for this Role

Name	Email	Phone
Title/Role	Company	

Name	Email	Phone
Title/Role	Company	

Name	Email	Phone
Title/Role	Company	

Name	Email	Phone
Title/Role	Company	

Notes, Feedback, Reflection, Any Questions that Need Followup

(1)—(2)—(3)—(4)—(5)—(6)—(7)—(8)—(9)

Application Sent Follow Up Sent Interview 1 Thank You Sent Interview 2 Interview 3 Offer Received Rejected Accepted

Position Title   Company Name   Glassdoor Rating

Date Applied   Deadline   Company Website

Salary   Address
$

Source/Reference #   Commute Time
                                                                 hh   mm

Website Login
u: p:
                                                                 ☐ Posted Directly
                                                                 ☐ Posted by Agency

Interviews

1 Date & Time   Location   Contact

Questions to Ask During Interview & Notes for Follow-Up

                                              ☐ Thank You Note Sent

2 Date & Time   Location   Contact

Questions to Ask During Interview & Notes for Follow-Up

3 Date & Time   Location   Contact

Questions to Ask During Interview & Notes for Follow-Up

Contacts for this Role

Name	Email	Phone
Title/Role	Company	

Name	Email	Phone
Title/Role	Company	

Name	Email	Phone
Title/Role	Company	

Name	Email	Phone
Title/Role	Company	

Notes, Feedback, Reflection, Any Questions that Need Followup

Made in the USA
Las Vegas, NV
11 February 2025

17931882R00052